T0209933

MARRIAGE
BY THE
BOOK

A Biblical Guide to a Successful Marriage

MARVIN L. BAGENT

WESTBOW
PRESS®
A DIVISION OF THOMAS NELSON
& ZONDERVAN

Copyright © 2018 Marvin L. Bagent.

All rights reserved. No part of this book may be used or reproduced by any means, graphic, electronic, or mechanical, including photocopying, recording, taping or by any information storage retrieval system without the written permission of the author except in the case of brief quotations embodied in critical articles and reviews.

This book is a work of non-fiction. Unless otherwise noted, the author and the publisher make no explicit guarantees as to the accuracy of the information contained in this book and in some cases, names of people and places have been altered to protect their privacy.

Scripture taken from the King James Version of the Bible.

WestBow Press books may be ordered through booksellers or by contacting:

WestBow Press
A Division of Thomas Nelson & Zondervan
1663 Liberty Drive
Bloomington, IN 47403
www.westbowpress.com
1 (866) 928-1240

Because of the dynamic nature of the Internet, any web addresses or links contained in this book may have changed since publication and may no longer be valid. The views expressed in this work are solely those of the author and do not necessarily reflect the views of the publisher, and the publisher hereby disclaims any responsibility for them.

Any people depicted in stock imagery provided by Getty Images are models, and such images are being used for illustrative purposes only. Certain stock imagery © Getty Images.

ISBN: 978-1-9736-3890-2 (sc)
ISBN: 978-1-9736-3889-6 (hc)
ISBN: 978-1-9736-3891-9 (e)

Library of Congress Control Number: 2018910553

Print information available on the last page.

WestBow Press rev. date: 9/12/2018

In memory of Dr. Lowell Davey, founder of Bible Broadcasting Network, my friend and mentor.

Why I Wrote This Book

Marriage is the foundation of society. It was instituted by God for everyone's benefit. God gave us a design for marriage that is being missed today. The almost 50 percent divorce rate is evidence of that fact.

I want the reader to understand God's pattern for marriage; we cannot follow what we do not know. If we follow God's plan, our marriages will succeed. My prayer is that your marriage will be successful.

Why You Should Read This Book

There are three groups of people who will benefit from reading this book. The unmarried should read it in preparation for marriage. Their first benefit will be found in preparing themselves for marriage. Then, the book will enable unmarried people to recognize a good candidate for marriage.

The second group that should read this book is married people. Most Christians today have never made a study of marriage from the Bible. This book will make it easy to understand the principles God has set forth for a solid marriage.

The third group of people who should read this book are those who perform marriage ceremonies. This book will provide a great platform upon which to base premarital counseling. Pastors will find great benefit as they help young couples prepare to take their wedding vows.

The purpose of this book is to provide a better understanding of what the Bible says about marriage.

CONTENTS

INTRODUCTION
The Benefits of Marriage

The purpose of this book is to help maintain the marital relationships.

Maintenance is easier if we understand the makeup of a biblical marriage. Those who are not married can use the information here as marriage counseling prior to getting married. They will get instruction about the purpose and the problems of marriage ahead of their wedding ceremony.

We want to begin our journey by listing the benefits of marriage. Knowing the benefits of marriage will motivate us to maintain our marriages.

1. Completion

The benefit here is mutual.

> Therefore shall a man leave his father and mother and shall cleave unto his wife and they shall be one flesh. (Genesis 2:24)

The husband gets a completer, someone who makes him a whole person, someone to share his life with and give him balance. That balance shows itself in many ways. The husband is strong, while the wife is vulnerable. The husband is logical, while his wife is intuitive. The husband is the leader, while his wife is his helper.

> And the LORD said, It is not good that the man should be alone: I will make an help meet for him. (Genesis 2:18)

The wife gets a champion. She gets someone to look up to and respect. She gets someone who will take up her cause and protect her. She gets someone who will love her.

> Nevertheless let every one of you in particular so love his wife even as himself: and the wife see that she reverence he husband. (Ephesians 5:33)

2. Companionship

The second benefit of marriage is companionship. Marriage is salvation from loneliness.

> And the LORD God said, it is not good that man should be alone. (Genesis 2:18)

Companionship means having someone to be with, someone to share with. We all need support from time to time. Marriage provides that support.

> Two are better than one. (Ecclesiastes 4:9)

3. Constraint

The next benefit of marriage is constraint. This is a moral issue.

Nevertheless, to avoid fornication, let every man
have his own wife, and let every woman have
her own husband. (1 Corinthians 7:2)

Marriage is an exclusive relationship. It serves as a moral constraint on society. Marriage's exclusiveness serves as a shield against social diseases. At the same time, marriage affords partners the freedom to enjoy one another physically and to have their physical needs met.

4. Consummation

The fourth benefit of marriage gives sexual relationships meaning and fulfillment.

Let thy fountain be blessed; and rejoice with
the wife of thy youth. (Proverbs 5:18)

Mutual satisfaction becomes the objective of physical relationships. Marriage brings a means of getting to know our mates in the most intimate way we know. And this relationship has no quilt.

Marriage is honourable in all, and the bed undefiled: but
whoremongers and adulters God will judge. (Hebrews 13:4)

5. Children

Children are the objective of marriage in God's economy.

And did not he make one? Yet had he the residue of the
spirit. That he might seek a Godly seed. (Malachi 2:15)

Children are not a burden. They are a blessing. They are the physical expression of oneness in marriage. They are a source of joy.

Lo children are an heritage of the LORD: and the
fruit of the womb is his reward. Happy is the man that
hath his quiver full of them. (Psalm 127:3–4)

6. Church

The church is described in the Bible as the "Body of Christ," and all
believers are members. The church is also described as the "Bride
of Christ." Marriage allows us to mirror the relationship of Christ
and the church.

For the husband is the head of the wife, even as Christ
is the head of the church. (Ephesians 5:23)

Husbands, love your wives, even as Christ also loved the
church, and gave himself for it. (Ephesians 5:25)

Marriage reflects the love of Christ for His church. It also mirrors the
churches submission to Christ. What a privilege marriage affords us.

Now, once we know the benefits of marriage, we are encouraged to
find out just what marriage is. That will compose the first chapter
of this book.

This is a book about marriage as it is outlined in the Bible. I do not
propose to tell you how to save your marriage but rather to give you
a picture of how the Bible describes what a marriage should be like.
My hope is that you will see the design that God has for marriage
and follow that design. If you do, you have a 100 percent chance of
your marriage being successful.

CHAPTER ONE
The Biblical Definition of Marriage

I want to begin with some common misconceptions about marriage. Each one of these misconceptions is a part (but not the whole concept) of marriage, according to the Bible.

Four Marriage Misconceptions

1. Marriage Is Not Just a Ceremony

A wedding ceremony is a beautiful thing. Most people believe that the ceremony is the essence of marriage, but as beautiful and meaningful as a wedding ceremony may be, it's not the essence of marriage. The wedding ceremony makes a marriage a matter of public record. Guests are witnesses, and there is a public declaration of union. But a ceremony by itself does not constitute a biblical marriage.

2. Marriage Is Not Just a Legal Contract

To be recognized by the government, a marriage requires a contract to be drawn up and signed by a government authority, the marriage participants, and witnesses. Biblically, then, the contract is necessary because Romans 13:1 says, "Let every soul be subject unto the higher powers. For there is no power but of God; the powers that be are ordained of God." A marriage would be neither legal nor blessed of God unless there was a contract made between a man and a woman. But the contract is not the essence of marriage. A contract is drawn up between two people basically because of distrust rather than because of trust for one another. Trust, of course, is the basis of a good marriage.

3. Marriage Is Not Just a Cohabitation

The trend among young people today is to live together and avoid the legal contract. There are many arguments made for this arrangement. Some point out that 50 percent of marriages fail. Others reason that you should try one another out to see whether you're compatible before signing a marriage contract. After all, no one would buy a car without driving it first. Of course, we realize that people are not things and cannot be tried out. One might further reason that marriage is essentially living together anyway, so what's the difference?

But there are some problems with this relationship. First, it lacks permanency. The Bible talks about marriage as "two becoming one flesh" (Genesis 2:24). This describes permanence and an intimacy that cannot be attained by cohabitation. Biblically, there is a far greater problem in that cohabitation, sexually, would constitute fornication. According to the biblical definition, fornication is the sin of having physical relations before marriage. 1 Corinthians 6:18 admonishes us to "flee fornication. Every sin that a man doeth is without the body; but he that committeth fornication sinneth against his own body." So biblically speaking, cohabitation is not the essence of marriage.

4. Marriage Is Not Just a Sexual Union

Today we hear young people say, "It's just sex." They seem to miss the real meaning of sexual union between a man and a woman. Living together without marriage vows and a contract lacks the commitment that brings permanence to a relationship. The Bible offers another view of the sexual union. It describes sexual union as the means of making two into one flesh. 1 Corinthians 6:16 says, "What? Know ye not that he which is joined to an harlot is one body? For two, saith he, shall be one flesh." According to Genesis 2:24, a sexual union is to be preceded by a "leaving and cleaving." This leaving of parents and cleaving to your mate establishes a new family unit. Sexual union is a significant and pleasurable part of marriage, but biblically, it's not the essence of marriage.

The Definition of Marriage

We have considered what marriage is not; now we want to determine what marriage is. Marriage as defined in the Bible is a little different than we might define it. Most folk think of marriage as a commitment, but that's not the word the Bible uses:

> Marriage is a lifelong, voluntary covenant made mutually between a man and a woman, witnessed by God and society.

The keyword in this definition is the word *covenant*. We find that word used in Malachi 2:14 referring to marriage. The verse says, "Yet ye say, Wherefore? Because the LORD hath been witness between thee and the wife of thy youth, against whom thou hast dealt treacherously; yet is she thy companion, and the wife of thy covenant." Marriage then is more than a commitment; it is a covenant.

3

The Definition of a Covenant

A covenant is a solemn, binding agreement between two parties, considered to be unchangeable.

There are basically two types of covenants spoken about in the Bible. The first is a covenant between God and humankind. God made such a covenant with Noah in Genesis 9:14–15: "And it shall come to pass, when I bring a cloud over the earth, that the bow shall be seen in the cloud; and I will remember my covenant, which is between me and you and every living creature of all flesh; and the waters shall no more become a flood to destroy all flesh."

The second type of covenant is one made between two people. An example of this type of covenant is the one set up between Jacob and his father-in-law, Laban, in Genesis 31:44–45: "'Now therefore come thou, let us make a covenant, I and thou; and let it be for a witness between me and thee.' And Jacob took a stone, and set it up for a pillar." Now let's look at the principal elements of a covenant and see how they are applied to a marriage covenant.

A Covenant Involves Stated, Agreed-Upon Terms

In marriage, the terms of the covenant are stated in the wedding vows. These vows should be read and agreed upon before the ceremony takes place. They must be thought about and approved by both parties. The vows I recommend to be used in a wedding ceremony are tried and true. I believe they are based on the scripture. They are to be repeated in the ceremony as an agreement and as a declaration of the stated responsibilities taken by both the bride and the groom.

Sample Vow Statements

The groom: "I, _____ _____, take thee, _____ _____, to be my wedded wife, to have and to hold from this day forward, for better, for worse, for richer, for poorer, in sickness and in health, to love and cherish, till death do us part."

The bride: "I, _____ _____, take thee, _____ _____, to be my wedded husband, to have and to hold from this day forward, for better, for worse, for richer, for poorer, in sickness and in health, to love and cherish, and obey, till death do us part."

Remember, God expects us to keep our vows. "When thou vowest a vow unto God, defer not to pay it; for he hath no pleasure in fools; pay that which thou hast vowed. Better is it that thou shouldest not vow, than that thou shouldest vow and not pay" (Ecclesiastes 5:4–5).

A Covenant Involves an Oath Made by Both Parties

According to *The American Heritage School Dictionary*, an oath is "a declaration or promise to act in a certain way, made with God or some other sacred object as witness." The wedding covenant includes an oath taken by both the bride and groom. This is a verbal agreement stated out loud for all the wedding witnesses to hear. We call them the "I do" statements. They are given by the minister or a justice of the peace, and these oaths are agreed to by the bride and groom individually by saying the words "I do."

Here are the "I do" statements as I would use them in a wedding ceremony. They are rhetorical statements, answered by the words "I do."

For the groom: "Will you have this woman to be your wedded wife, will you love her, honor her, and keep her, in sickness and in health, in poverty and in wealth, and forsaking all others, keep thee only unto her, so long as you both shall live?"

For the bride: "Will you have this man to be your wedded husband, will you love him, honor and keep him, in sickness as in health, in poverty as in wealth, and forsaking all others, keep thee only unto him so long as you both shall live?"

A Covenant Involves a Formal Ratification

To ratify something is to verify it or make it officially valid, such as in the ratification of the Constitution of the United States by the several states officially making the Constitution valid. The covenant was usually ratified by a public ceremony and by the exchange of a symbol of that covenant. The symbol of the wedding covenant has become the wedding ring. During the wedding ceremony, rings are exchanged between the bride and the groom. The ring is thought to symbolize eternity, but this is not the case in a marriage. A marriage covenant is limited: "until death do us part." Marriage is for life; it is not for eternity. The ring is a validation of the marriage covenant.

A Covenant Involves Witnesses

Witnesses are important in any legal situation. They verify and authenticate the covenant. The marriage covenant requires witnesses to make it valid, both legally and spiritually. At least two witnesses are required to make a covenant legal. At the wedding, these witnesses consist of the invited guests of both the bride and groom, and God himself. The Bible acknowledges the presence of God at a wedding; it is at the wedding that God joins the bride and groom together. "Wherefore they are no more twain, but one flesh. What therefore God hath joined together, let not man put asunder" (Matthew 19:5).

A Covenant Involves a Mediator

Mediators are people who bring two parties into agreement. They are authorized officiates of the government. They can be a duly authorized ministers, justices of the peace, judge, or even ship's captains. The mediator is able to declare the wedded couple to be man and wife.

A marriage then must be understood to be a lifelong covenant made before God and a duly recognized representative of the government. It should not be entered into lightly but with prayer and an assurance of God's will. God's will can be determined by God's peace, a "peace which passes all understanding" (Philippians 4:6).

CHAPTER TWO
The Seven Purposes of Marriage

Marriage was invented by God. When He instituted marriage, He had a plan. God had seven purposes in mind for this most intimate of relationships. We want to detail those purposes here.

Marriage Is for Perfection

When God created Adam, He soon realized something was missing. His creation was deemed "good," but man was not complete in himself. So God created a woman from one of Adam's ribs. This made the man complete in the marriage relationship.

> And the LORD God caused a deep sleep to fall upon Adam, and he slept: and he took one of his ribs, and closed up the flesh instead thereof; and the rib which the LORD God had taken from man, made he a woman, and he brought her unto the man. And Adam said, this is now bone of my bone, and flesh of my flesh. She shall be called woman, because she was taken out of man. (Genesis 2:21–23)

The need in Adam's life was met. Perfection was attained in the union of the man and the woman. Adam and Eve were innocent and without sin. The marriage was perfect. Each one was devoted to meeting the needs of the other and pleasing God, their Creator.

Marriage Is for Partnership

Marriage makes a couple complete. But also establishes a partnership. These two can work together to accomplish great things for God.

And the lord God said, It is not good that the man should be alone; I will make him a help meet for him. (Genesis 2:18)

Adam needed a helper. God provided not another man, but a woman, to help him. The woman was made to aid the man in his accomplishments, as God gave them direction.

Two are better than one; because they have a good reward for their labour. (Ecclesiastes 4:9)

The woman is not to be a servant. She is to share in their corporate success. Two are better than one.

Marriage Is for Prevention

God's purpose in instituting marriage was to prevent moral corruption on the earth. Every man was to have his own wife, and every woman was to have her own husband. Sexual relations outside of marriage, fornication, are not allowed.

Nevertheless, to avoid fornication, let every man have his own wife, and let every woman have her own husband. (1 Corinthians 7:2)

Marriage was to prevent moral impurity. Physical relations inside marriage are holy and good. But sex outside marriage is a sin. It is a sin against our own bodies, because fornication interrupts the oneness of the marriage union.

> Flee fornication. Every sin that a man doeth is without
> the body; but he that committeth fornication sinneth
> against his own body. (1 Corinthians 6:18)

Marriage is also a blessing to society. Social diseases are rampant among those immoral segments of our population. Marriage prevents contracting and spreading those diseases.

Marriage Is for Protection

Marriage is all about preventing the dangers and harm that could come to the family. The husband protects his wife from physical harm. The wife protects her home from evil influences as she censors the media that enters her home. Parents protect their children from the defilement of wrong friendships and the occasional bully at school.

> And did not he make one? Yet had he the residue of
> the spirit, that he might seek a godly seed. Therefore
> take heed to you spirit, and let none deal treacherously
> against the wife of thy youth. (Malachi 2:15)

Marriage Is for Pleasure

The single life can be very lonely. God instituted marriage so two people could find real joy and happiness in each other's fellowship. He intended pleasure to be part of the physical relationship of marriage. The mutual meeting of one another's needs would thus last a lifetime.

> Let the fountain be blessed, and rejoice with
> the wife of thy youth. (Proverbs 5:18)

This pleasure brings no guilt; the act of marriage is totally sanctioned by God. The meeting of those physical desires is God's gift to those married according to his plan.

> Marriage is honorable in all, and the bed undefiled: but
> whoremongers and adulterers God will judge. (Hebrews 13:4)

Marriage Is for Procreation

One of the main purposes of marriage is to bring children into this world. God intended marriage to be the means of replenishing the earth and populating the planet. The number of children each family should have may be debated. But the word *replenish* means to do more than just replace ourselves. The number of children needed to replenish the earth would then begin at three, two to replace ourselves and one more to replenish the earth.

> And God blessed them, and God said unto them, be fruitful,
> and multiply, and replenish the earth, and have dominion over
> the fish of the sea, and over the fowl of the air, and over every
> living thing that moveth upon the earth. (Genesis 1:28)

Children are not a burden but a blessing. Children are the heritage of the Lord and His reward given to us. Marriage is the context for raising children, and they are the source of great happiness.

> Lo children are the heritage of the LORD; and the fruit
> of the womb is his reward. As arrows are in the hand of a
> mighty man; so are the children of the youth. Happy is the
> man that hath his quiver full of them. (Psalm 127:3–5)

Children, like the arrows in the hand of a mighty man, send a message to the world. Rightly raised, they become a godly influence on our sinful world.

Marriage Is for Picturing Christ

We generally think of Christ as God in the flesh, the Savior of the world, and the coming King of Israel. But in our age, Christ is the husband of His bride, the church. Marriage reflects the love Christ has for His church.

> Husbands, love your wives, even as Christ loved the church and gave himself for it. (Ephesians 5:25)

Marriage pictures the church's submission to its head, the Lord Jesus Christ, just as the wife submits to the leadership of her husband.

For the husband is the head of the wife, even as Christ is the head of the church; and he is the saviour of the body. (Ephesians 5:23)

> Therefore as the church is subject unto Christ, so let the wives be to their own husbands in everything. (Ephesians 5:24)

Marriage is founded on these seven purposes. God's wisdom is made evident as we live together in holy matrimony. We want to work with God as He fulfills these purposes through our marriages.

CHAPTER THREE
The Role of the Husband

Introduction

God works through a chain of command. He is the ultimate authority in the universe. God delegates His authority in every area of life.

> Let every soul be subject to the higher powers.
> For there is no power but of God; the powers
> that be ordained of God. (Romans 13:1)

God's order of authority in the family is presented in 1 Corinthians 11:3. This chain of command begins with God, then Christ, then the husband, then the wife, and after that the children.

> But I would have you to know, that the head of every man is Christ; and the head of the woman is the man; and the head of Christ is God. (1 Corinthians 11:3)

The roles in marriage are played according to the chain of command as it is presented here. I want to share both the role of the husband and the role of the wife in marriage as they are presented in the Bible. I believe if people understand their unique role and play that role, their marriage will be successful. I will begin with the role of the husband.

1. The Husband Is the Leader

> The husband is the head of the wife, even as Christ is the head of the church, and the saviour of the body. (Ephesians 5:23)

The husband is the head of the wife. The head makes the final decisions. There can be only one head. Anything with two heads would be a monster. This means the husband takes the responsibility for the final decisions. If a couple decide to buy a used car, and it turns out to be a lemon, the husband is responsible for the lemon.

The husband, as the leader of his wife and family, bears responsibility in several areas. First, he is responsible spiritually. Often, the spiritual leader in the home is the wife. This ought not to be so. The responsibility spiritually means moving the family closer to God. This is done through a godly example and directing the family to a good Bible-believing church.

The husband is also responsible for financial leadership. He and not his wife is responsible for making and managing the money. The wife may add to the family income, but the responsibility is the husband's.

Couples often make the mistake of allowing the wife to manage the family finances. She then becomes the controller and bears the responsibility for spending the family's money. The responsible wife may pay all the bills, not leaving any money for groceries, but the bills will be paid. This is a pressure and a position that God intends for the husband to bear. God has given husbands the temperament to handle these matters.

The husband is also responsible for the education and training of the children. Final decisions about how and where to educate the children are his responsibility as the head of the household. These decisions can be made together, but the final decision is the husband's as the leader of the family.

2. The Husband Is the Lover

> Husbands, love your wives, even as Christ also loved the
> church, and gave himself for it. (Ephesians 5:25)

The husband must love his wife. This is God's command. Love is not just an emotion. Love is a decision. Husbands are to love their wives as Christ loved the church.

Christ's love for the church was sacrificial. He gave his life for the church. Real love gives and sacrifices. The husband is to give his life for his wife. Not just physically, but in practical, self-sacrificing ways.

Love then is the basis of leadership. A loving husband will find little resistance to his leadership in the home.

3. The Husband Is the Provider

> But if any provide not for his own, and specially for
> those of his own house, he hath denied the faith,
> and is worse than an infidel. (1 Timothy 5:8)

The husband is responsible for providing the basic needs of the family, including food, clothing, and shelter. He provides these needs by work. He must manage the money to see that it meets the needs. By diligently budgeting and being responsible for every penny, he will succeed in providing for his wife and family.

4. The Husband Is the Protector

> Likewise, ye husbands, dwell with them according to
> knowledge, giving honour unto the wife, as unto the
> weaker vessel, and as being heirs together of the grace of
> life; that your prayers be not hindered. (1 Peter 3:7)

The husband is the protector of his wife and his family. The wife is described here as the "weaker vessel." This is referring to the contrast in the physical makeup of a man versus a woman. She needs protection against anyone who would harm her or her children. This protection extends to three areas.

The husband is charged with physically protecting his wife. Her physical safety is his responsibility. She should be protected from the danger of home intruders, or anything that would endanger her physically.

Not only is he charged with keeping her physically safe, he is also to protect her emotionally. He must keep her from undue stress and involvement in areas outside her area of responsibility.

Finally, the husband is responsible for morally protecting his wife and family. He is to monitor the immoral influences by the media and guard against the wrong influence of bad friendships. He should monitor the computers, books, and magazines in the home. He would, of course, censor any immoral content.

God has given huge responsibility to the husband as the head of the wife and family. His role is determined by those responsibilities. How well he plays his role will determined how good a husband and father he is.

CHAPTER FOUR
The Role of the Wife

Introduction

The simplest definition of a wife is "a married woman." But she will be much more than that to her husband. She will be his ally and confidant, as well as his partner and friend.

> And the LORD God said, It is not good that the man should be alone: I will make an help meet for him. (Genesis 2:18)

The value of a good wife is multifold. The Bible describes her value in several ways.

First, a wife is a good thing.

> Whoso findeth a wife findeth a good thing. (Proverbs 18:22)

Second, a wife's value is above rubies.

> Who can find a virtuous woman? For her price
> is far above rubies. (Proverbs 31:10)

Third, a wife completes her husband.

Therefore shall a man leave his father and his mother, and shall cleave unto his wife; and they shall be one flesh. (Genesis 2:24)

While the wife was made to be a helper, playing her role will not be easy. Her natural desire will be to control her husband. The wife must guard against the desire to be in charge and yield to her husband's leadership.

Unto the woman he said, I will greatly multiply thy sorrow and thy conception; in sorrow thou shalt bring forth children, and thy desire shall be to thy husband, and he shall rule over thee. (Genesis 3:16)

The wife's role in marriage involves four responsibilities. Let's look at them now.

1. The Wife Must Submit to Her Husband

Submission means to be under authority. God is the ultimate authority. He delegates that authority by way of a chain of command.

But I would have you to know, that the head of every man is Christ; and the head of the woman is the man; and the head of Christ is God. (1 Corinthians 11:2)

Submission has two bases:

First, the order of creation.

But I suffer not a woman to teach, nor usurp authority over the man, but to be in silence. For Adam was first formed then Eve. (1 Timothy 2:12–13)

Second, the origin of sin.

> And Adam was not deceived, but the woman being
> deceived was in the transgression. (1 Timothy 2:14)

Based on these two events, the wife is bound to submit to her husband. This does not make her a slave, but she must be under the authority of her husband when final decisions are made.

Submission is to be in her spirit.

> But let it be in the hidden man of the heart, in that which is
> not corruptible, even the ornament of a meek and quiet spirit,
> which is in the site of God of great price. (1 Peter 3:4)

A wife's submission has a twofold purpose. First, so that the Word of God is not blasphemed or degraded.

> To be discreet, chaste, keepers at home, good,
> obedient to their own husbands, that the word
> of God be not blasphemed. (Titus 2:5)

The second purpose is that an unsaved husband may be won to the Lord. A rebellious wife would have little hope of seeing her husband converted.

> Like wise, ye wives be in subjection to your own husbands;
> that, if any obey not the word, they also may without the
> word be won by the conversation of the wives. (1 Peter 3:1)

If a wife refuses to submit to the authority of her husband, it could very well bring disaster to herself. Her children could also suffer.

> Every wise woman buildeth her house; but the foolish
> plucketh it down with hands. (Proverbs 14:1)

When a wife takes matters into her own hands and rebels against her husband's wishes, she risks destroying her home. Her children will also be affected by the duel authority set up in such a situation.

2. The Wife Must Counsel Her Husband

Counseling is not nagging. Counsel is the advice of a friend.

> It is better to dwell in a corner of the house top, than with
> a brawling woman in a wide house. (Proverbs 21:9)

Counsel is important in any endeavor. It gives us perspective and a different point of view. Often success is achieved and failure is avoided by listening to good counsel.

> For by wise counsel thou shalt make thy war: and in a
> multitude of counselors there is safety. (Proverbs 24:6)

A wife's counsel will often be confusing to her husband because it may be based on intuition. God has given insight to women, and they intuitively know when something is amiss. Pilate's wife gave him such advice about the crucifixion of Christ.

> When he was set down on the judgment seat, his wife
> sent unto him saying, have nothing to do with that
> just man; for I have suffered many things this day
> in a dream because of him. (Matthew 27:19)

There is a limit to a wife's responsibility to be in subjection to her husband. That limit is sin. If she is asked to violate God's will, she is obligated to "obey God rather than men" (Acts 5:29).

Before refusing to do what is biblically inappropriate, the wife should make an appeal to her husband. She should explain why she feels the action is wrong and ask to be allowed not to participate. If this fails, she will suffer the consequences. We must obey God.

3. The Wife Must Revere Her Husband

What men want more than anything else in life is respect: respect from his family, his friends, his coworkers, and his wife.

> Nevertheless let every one of you in particular so
> love his wife even as himself; and the wife see that
> she reverence her husband. (Ephesians 5:33)

That reverence and respect is to last a lifetime. A wife is to maintain such respect, even after her husband is dead.

> She will do him good and not evil all the
> days of her life. (Proverbs 3:12)

The wife's reverence for her husband is based on his position as the head of the family. This attitude is possible by giving her expectations to God. She should expect God to give direction to her husband and to change him, if necessary.

4. The Wife Must Be a Keeper at Home

The fourth responsibility of the wife is difficult in this day of equality and equal rights. Women are a part of the workforce in our society. But the scripture is clear: one of the roles of the wife is to be a keeper at home.

> The aged women likewise, that they be in behaviour as becometh
> holiness, not false accusers, not given to much wine, teachers of
> good things; that they may teach the young women to be sober,
> to love their husbands, to love their children, to be discreet,

chaste, keepers at home, good, obedient to their own husbands, that the word of God be not blasphemed. (Titus 2:3–5)

The home consists of a house and the family. A home equals a lot of work to keep clean and functioning so the needs of the husband and children are met. The home is important to the family; it's a place of learning. Children are taught the basics of obedience and respect. The home is a retreat from the rest of the world. It should be a place of joy and rejoicing. It should be a little piece of heaven on the earth, where the family can enjoy one another.

Roles in marriage make the marriage run efficiently and effectively. These roles bring honor to God. They serve to enhance His design for marriage success.

CHAPTER FIVE
The Foundation of Marriage

The foundation of any giant building is immensely important. The foundation must be dug first; before going up, you have to go down. The stability of marriage has a similar pattern. Stability and success are dependent on the foundation of the marriage.

> If the foundation be destroyed what can
> the righteous do? (Psalm 11:3)

There are seven qualities that form the foundation of marriage. These qualities are what makes a marriage last. If they are absent, the marriage will be shaky at best. These qualities should be developed before the couple gets married. Our goal should be to develop these qualities while we are waiting to find the one God wants us to have in marriage. These traits will qualify us as good marriage material.

Let's look closely at these seven qualities of character that make a marriage stable and lasting.

1. Love

Love is difficult to define. I once made a study of love in the Bible and wrote out a definition. After I considered my definition, I saw that it wasn't a definition; it was a description. Love is much easier to describe than to define. Love is a verb. Love acts.

The Bible says, "God is love." The nature of love is to give.

> For God so loved the world, that he gave his only begotten Son, that whosoever believeth in him should not perish, but have eternal life. (John 3:16)

Love is described in 1 Corinthians 13:4–7. If you can read these verses and replace "love" with "I," you can believe you are in love with them.

> "I" suffer long, and "I" am kind, "I" envy not, "I" vaunt not myself, "I" am not puffed up, "I" do not behave unseemly, "I" seek not my own, "I" am not easily provoked, "I" think no evil, "I" rejoice not in iniquity, but "I" rejoice in the truth, "I" bear all things, "I" hope all things, "I" endure all things. (1 Corinthians 13:4–7)

Love is a decision of the will. We decide to love. It is an expression of emotion. But sometimes, the emotion of love is difficult to understand because we say we love God, and at the same time, we say we love pizza. Somehow, that doesn't equate.

The importance of love in marriage cannot be overstated. Husbands and wives are commanded to love one another.

> Husbands, love your wives. (Ephesians 5:25)

> That they may teach the young women to be sober, to love their husbands. (Titus 2:4)

Love is the bond of marriage. It is not the law or a valid marriage certificate that hold a marriage together. It is love. Love deepens with time and exercise. It is the emotional glue that helps a husband and wife stay together over the years.

Love meets needs. Love helps, comforts, consoles, and encourages. Love meets our physical needs, as well. Love provides food, clothing, and shelter for the loved ones. Love shares the most intimate of physical needs to make marriage a very satisfying relationship.

Love can be rekindled.

> Nevertheless I have somewhat against thee; because thou hast left thy first love, remember therefore from whence thou art fallen: and repent and do the first works. (Revelation 2:4–5)

The steps to rekindle a cold love are to first remember what love was like and to determine to regain that love. Second, repent; repentance is changing your mind. You must decide to love. Love is a decision, not just a feeling. Finally, return; that simply means to do what love does and has always done.

Love is essential in the marriage relationship. But there are six other qualities upon which marriage is built. Let's continue to consider those qualities.

2. Deference

The second quality necessary for a lasting marriage is deference. Deference means to give way to someone else's desires or preferences. It can be defined as respectful submission or yielding to the judgment, opinion, or will of another. The biblical example is Apostle Paul.

To the weak became I weak that I might gain the
weak; I am made all things to all men, that I might
by all means save some. (1 Corinthians 9:22)

One of the main benefits of deference is during the period of
marital adjustment. When two people come together from different
backgrounds, having different temperaments, it is difficult to become
one, as the Bible predicts will happen in marriage.

Therefore shall a man leave his father and his
mother, and shall cleave unto his wife; and they
shall become one flesh. (Genesis 2:24)

When we have differences of opinion and need to decide what to
do, deference is necessary. A willingness to defer to our mate's desire
will allow us to avoid many ugly disagreements. Sometimes, couples
get married with the erroneous idea that they will change their mate
after marriage. We can change, but only God can change us. Our
part is to give our expectations of change to him.

My soul, wait thou only upon God: for my
expectation is from him. (Psalm 62:5)

Deference helps us accept each other the way we are. Otherwise, we
must be patient to wait on God to change what needs to be changed.

3. Trust

The third quality necessary for a strong marital foundation is trust.
Trust is simply placing your confidence in another person. When a
couple is married, they put their confidence in one another. They
expect that they'll be told the truth and that obligations will be met.
They trust that the relationship will be kept exclusive. If this trust is
violated, the marriage will be damaged.

Who can find a virtuous woman? For her price is far above rubies. The heart of her husband doth safely trust in her, so that he shall have no need of spoil. (Proverbs 3:10–11)

Trust is important in marriage for several reasons.

A. Trust Eliminates Jealousy

Jealousy is often called a "green-eyed monster." I don't know if it has green eyes, but I do know that jealousy is a monster. Jealousy is a symptom of distrust and a sign of the possibility of unfaithfulness.

Wrath is cruel, and anger is outrageous; but who is able to stand before envy? (Proverbs 27:4; "envy" here is jealousy)

B. Trust Is Basic to Cooperation

We cannot work together unless we can trust one another.

Can two walk together, except they be agreed? (Amos 3:3)

Marriage brings two people together to build their lives together. Trust is needed as they cooperate in building a home, a family, and a life.

C. Trust Is Required for Intimacy

In marriage, we become one, both emotionally and physically. After years together, people even begin to look alike. To be meaningful and fulfilling, physical intimacy must be based on confidence, faithfulness, and exclusiveness.

The implementation of trust requires that each person is and remains trustworthy. This requires consistency. It may seem boring as we go through the adjustment period, but coming home on time, communicating our whereabouts, and maintaining a consistent schedule are all necessary to build a sense of trustworthiness.

We also need to be truthful. This simply means we can't lie to each other. We have to tell the truth, even if it hurts. Believe me, it might hurt now to tell the truth, but if we lie, it'll be disastrous later on, after the truth comes out. We should not only be truthful; we must also be honest. We may not lie, but we may not tell the whole truth. To be honest means that we must admit our failures. This isn't easy on our egos, but to maintain someone's trust, we must live in reality. Finally, to be trustworthy, we must be humble. We must admit when we mess up and ask forgiveness. Trust is a fundamental quality of a stable marriage.

4. Dependence

Dependence is relying on one another for needed help. Another way to define it is being sustained by another. In the Lord's Prayer, we are taught to pray these words: "Give us this day our daily bread." Dependence, not independence, is required to make a marriage strong.

Dependence is important for several reasons:

A. Dependence Is the Basis of Roles in Marriage

A husband is responsible as the provider. His wife is primarily responsible as the keeper of the home. While these roles can be supplemented by the other, we look to husbands and wives to care for their roles. Thus, we become dependent on each other.

B. Dependence Is the Basis of Gratitude

A wife is appreciated for meeting the needs of her husband. A husband is appreciated for meeting the needs of his wife.

C. Independence Is the First Step to Disloyalty

Independence by a husband or a wife simply says, "I don't need you." Independence has become easier today because men can cook and women can work.

So the only question left is, how can we implement dependence? First, we must look to our mate to fulfill his or her role. We must be careful not to switch roles. This would bring only confusion. Finally, don't allow anyone else to fulfill your mate's role.

5. Forgiveness

One of the most important qualities marriage is founded on is forgiveness. Forgiveness is releasing someone of a debt. When you offend someone, you come into their debt. You owe them; they own you. We cannot live with someone without offending them.

> For in many things we offend all. If any man offend
> not in word, the same is a perfect man, and able
> also to bridle the whole body. (James 3:2)

There are several keys to implementing forgiveness.

First, we must understand the true offense. We may have said something offensive. We may have expressed a wrong attitude, or we may have simply been inconsiderate. Just make sure you know exactly what the offense was.

Second, before you apologize, work out what you will say. Know exactly what you're going to say when you seek forgiveness.

Third, speak directly to the offended party. You may use the phone, but don't document your apology in a letter. Unless it is not possible to come face to face, a letter could be used against you if the apology is not accepted.

Fourth, ask forgiveness. Use the specific words "Will you forgive me?" Don't just say, "I'm sorry." That does not request forgiveness.

Finally, wait for an answer. If you're told you are forgiven, you're released from your debt. The issue then is resolved.

Getting forgiveness is not end of the story. We must now rebuild that relationship. Communicate your feelings, humble yourself, and rebuild that relationship.

6. Humor

Humor is useful because it can break the tension in a difficult situation. The ability to laugh at yourself and to make others laugh without offending them has great value in marriage. We must be careful not to use sarcasm. We don't want to belittle others or ridicule anyone. That is not true humor.

> A merry heart maketh a cheerful countenance: but by
> sorrow of heart the spirit is broken. (Proverbs 15:13)

7. Kindness

Kindness is the expression of consideration. Kindness is the basis of good manners and the evidence of unselfishness.

And be ye kind one to another, tenderhearted,
forgiving one another, even as God for Christ's
sake hath forgiven you. (Ephesians 4:32)

When implementing kindness, it's important to do the little things. A caring word, a warm smile, a gentle hug all go a long way toward making others feel loved. Kindness asks the question, "How are you doing?" When others are hurting, kindness is concerned. A kind word is worth its weight in gold to someone who is hurting.

Conclusion

These seven qualities form the foundation of a strong and lasting marriage. Now we continue to a subject of equal importance: communication in marriage.

CHAPTER SIX
Communication in Marriage

Introduction

Marriage has three danger zones: communication, money, and sex. Couples must conquer all three of these danger zones to have a successful marriage. This chapter will detail one of those zones: communication. Intimacy is built on the ability to communicate with one another. These three areas cause the majority of problems in marriage. They are the leading issues that lead to divorce. We will deal with money problems and sexual problems later in the book. But we want to deal with the problem of proper communication first of all.

The Importance of Communication

What really holds a marriage together? Physical attraction is powerful, but it fades over time; love is important, but the real glue of marriage is communication. Couples who can talk to one another and work out their problem are the ones who stick together over time.

As a matter of fact, statistics show that problems stemming from poor communication cause the most couples to divorce. One would not think that something as simple as talking could cause a problem large enough to separate a couple, but it can. So let's talk about the art of communication.

The Meaning of Communication

Communication is a skill. A skill is something we learn to do. Typists, pianists, plumbers, and surgeons all had to learn their skills. Communication, then, is something we can get better at by doing.

> A word fitly spoken is like apples of gold in
> pictures of silver. (Proverbs 25:11)

Communication is sharing information. This is done by talking. We first must share information. Then we may ask questions to get clarification.

A good part of communication is listening. A good listener is a good communicator. Communication, then, is the art of making yourself understood and understanding others. Communication is useful in many areas.

The Purpose of Communication

Good communication skills have many benefits. First, it promotes understanding. Communication clarifies issues. In order to solve a problem in marriage, it must be understood. Once the difficulties are understood, they can be confronted and then settled. We can't ignore our problems in marriage. They must be solved.

Communication also promotes intimacy. Intimacy is sharing your whole life with your mate. To attain this type of intimacy, we must talk to each other. Being quiet may be okay, but not in marriage.

The Means of Communication

Recent generations have added some new means of communication: smart phones, texting, tweeting, and posting are all new to my generation. The old-school forms of communication, however, still work. The spoken word is still effective. It is still the first means of communication, but we must be careful with our words.

> In the multitude of words there wanteth not sin; but he that refraineth his lips is wise. (Proverbs 10:19

Gestures and facial expression are effective ways to communicate without speaking. A smile sends a message, while a frown says you're not happy. A finger to the lips will tell you to stop talking.

Writing is a lost art today, but it's still a time-honored and effective way to express ourselves. It seems love letters stop coming as soon as we go down the wedding aisle.

The Process of Communication

I am grateful to Dr. James Dobson for his advice on the process of communication. I was trying to explain the process of communication to my young son. Dr. Dobson's illustration was from baseball, which was helpful, because my son was into baseball. Dr. Dobson said, "When someone speaks to you, it is like playing catch. You're expected to throw the ball back."

Communication has four elements. First, there is a sender, the speaker. Second is the receiver, the listener. Third is the message; this is the information to be communicated. Finally, there is a response. The response is the message sent back to the original speaker.

The process of communication is simple: A message is sent. The content is heard. A meaning is assigned. A reply is formed, and the receiver of the message responds. As Dr. Dobson said, "Catch the ball and throw it back."

Communication Breakers

In marriage, there are three common communication breakers. We must always be aware of the damage these actions can bring.

1. Anger

This is usually a problem for men. Men tend to explode in anger, saying and doing things they wish they had not. Women can get mad but are usually not as explosive as men.

2. Tears

Men usually are not guilty of tears, but ladies are. Crying is often a defensive ploy for women to get their way. Men should try to understand a woman's tears. When a woman cries, it could be tears of joy, but it's more often an expression of frustration. Tears for a woman are often a release of tension. Men must evaluate the function of the tears. Sympathy may be the needed response.

3. Silence

Both men and women can be guilty of silence. This means we simply do not respond. Silence is an attempt to avoid a confrontation. This doesn't solve anything; it only serves to frustrate our mate.

The Golden Phrases of Communication

There are three golden phrases that must be deployed in every successful marriage. They are difficult to say, but used properly, they will solve a multitude of problems.

The first phrase is "I love you." Before my wife and I were married, her father once said to me, "My daughter is not sure you love her." I said to him, "Well, she should be; I told her once that I did." This phrase must be used over and over again by both mates. "I love you" reassures your mate of your love. It is a declaration of affection. It cannot be said too often.

The second phrase is "I am sorry." This phrase admits quilt. It must be used when we have offended our mates. It also expresses humility. We must humble ourselves if we expect to be forgiven. Pride always leads to destruction.

> Pride goeth before destruction, and an haughty
> spirit before a fall. (Proverbs 16:18)

The third phrase is "Will you forgive me?" This phrase leads to a release from debt: not a financial debt, but an emotional debt caused by an offence. It is a request that assumes no response, but if granted, it ends any argument. When I was young, my parents often argued over things that had happened years ago. They had never said the words, "Will you forgive me?" Their relationship had been damaged and never restored. This phrase restores a relationship, like magic.

The Rules of a "Good" Fight

In marriage, there are times when we have disagreements and issues that must be addressed for the good of the marriage. Sometimes, we may even have an argument. A fight can be a good thing, if there is a good result.

The question is, How do you have a good fight? Here are some instructions to follow as we try to have a good fight:

1. How to Start

Don't start a fight after ten o'clock at night. It's too late. You are tired. You don't have time to finish. Wait until tomorrow. Realize the source of contention is always pride. Make sure your problem is not based on selfishness.

> Only by pride cometh contention: but with the
> well advised is wisdom. (Proverbs 13:10)

Fight only over important issues. The fact that your husband never puts his dirty socks in the hamper may not be an issue worthy of a fight. If there is an important issue, confront the problem. Clarify the issue, and settle the differences.

2. How to Settle

First, stick to the issue. Don't let yourself get off track.

Second, listen and try to understand what the issue is. Sometimes, a problem develops simply because we don't understand it.

> He that answereth a matter before he heareth it; it is
> a folly and shame unto him. (Proverbs 18:13)

Third, we must "speak the truth in love." Sometimes, the truth does hurt. The truth spoken with the benefit of the offender in mind has great results.

> But speaking the truth in love, may grow up into him in all
> things which is the head, even Christ. (Ephesians 4:15)

Finally, don't lose your temper. Anger leads to sin and a bad result. If things get emotional, take a little break. Be careful not to use abusive language. Don't resort to name calling. Words like "lazy," "stubborn," and "uncaring" can be as counterproductive as curse words. Such words never belong in a good fight.

3. How to Stop

If you realize that you were wrong or need to do better, admit it.

> He that covereth his sins shall not prosper; but whoso confesseth and forsaketh them shall have mercy. (Proverbs 28:13)

All arguments must be settled before you go to sleep. You don't want to have a continuing problem. You won't sleep well, anyway, if the fight isn't concluded.

> Be ye angry and sin not; let not the sun go down upon your wrath. (Ephesians 4:26)

Finally, don't forget to ask forgiveness. If you are the offender and want to do better, great, but clear the record: ask forgiveness. This brings closure. The issue is resolved. You have had a good fight.

> And be kind one to another, tender hearted, forgiving one another, even as God for Christ's sake hath forgiven you. (Ephesians 4:32)

Finally, let me say communication is supremely important in marriage. It takes work. We are not all great communicators, but every improvement is worth it. Now it is on to another danger zone: sex in marriage.

Chapter Seven
Sex in Marriage

The second danger zone in marriage is the area of sex. Sex is a principal part of marriage. It is a source of unparalleled intimacy. But big problems can be associated with this most intimate part of marriage. Many marriages end upon the rocks because of mistakes and miscues in this area.

We want to help you understand what the Bible teaches about the proper handling of sex in marriage. We don't plan on giving advice, only instructions given by God.

The Biblical Attitude toward Sex

1. Sex Is Good

God is the Creator of everything. When the six days of creation were finished, His evaluation was that it was "good." Sex was one of the things God included in his creation of Adam and Eve.

> And God saw every thing that he made, and
> behold, it was very good. (Genesis 1:31)

2. Sex Is More Than a Biological Drive

The sexual drives and desires we have are natural. God made us this way. His intention for the sex drive was that it would be an expression of oneness in marriage.

Therefore shall a man leave his father and his mother, and shall cleave unto his wife; and they shall be one flesh. (Genesis 2:24)

3. Sex Is Not Immoral

Sex can be immoral if done outside the bonds of marriage. Marriage is where God intended for it to be. Inside marriage, sex is wholesome and undefiled, but when relations take place between unmarried people, it can bring judgment from God.

Marriage is honorable in all, and the bed undefiled; but whoremongers and adulterers God will judge. (Hebrews 13:4)

4. Sex Is a Mutual Responsibility

The sexual desires we have are to be met by our mates. The husband is to meet the desires of his wife. The wife is to meet the needs of her husband. We have a mutual responsibility.

Let the husband render unto the wife due benevolence; and likewise also the wife unto her husband. The wife hath not power of her own body, but the husband; and likewise also the husband hath not power of his own body, but the wife. (1 Corinthians 7: 3–4)

The Biblical Purposes of Sex

1. Procreation

God wants children to come into this world. To succeed, children need a family. The sex drive aids this purpose.

> And God blessed them, and God said unto them, be fruitful, and multiply and replenish the earth. (Genesis 1:28)

2. Pleasure

God planned a way to attract and motivate couples to marry. Physical relations are pleasurable. We need not to be embarrassed or apologetic about these emotions.

> Let thy fountain be blessed, and rejoice with
> the wife of thy youth. (Proverbs 5:18)

3. Intimacy

Intimacy is about knowing one another really well. The deepest way to know someone is to know them physically. This act is a part of the marital relationship. By this act, a couple gets to know each other in the deepest way possible.

> And Adam knew Eve his wife; and she conceived, and bare Cain, and said, I have gotten a man from the LORD. (Genesis 4:1)

4. Purity

Purity is first personal. Marriage insures sexual purity. It serves to protect a couple from social diseases. Sexually transmitted diseases would not be a problem if there were no illicit sexual activity. This would be a protection for all of society.

Nevertheless, to avoid fornication, let every man have his own wife, and let every woman have her own husband. (1 Corinthians 7:2)

The Biblical Boundaries of Sex

God designed sex for marriage only, no exceptions. Sex can be perverted in two ways; first, by committing adultery. Adultery happens after marriage. Adultery is having sexual relations with someone other than your mate.

Thou shalt not commit adultery. (Exodus 20:14)

Second, sex can be perverted by fornication. Fornication is illicit sex before marriage. It is a broad word that can include adultery and every other form of illicit sexual activity. The Bible prohibits both adultery and fornication.

Flee fornication. Every sin that a man doeth is without the body: but he that committeth fornication sinneth against his own body. (1 Corinthians 6:18)

Practical Principles of Sex

Sex has a different meaning to husbands and a wives. Sex satisfies a husband's sexual drive. His hormones peak early, and his wife can satisfy those desires. Sex fulfills his feelings of manhood and at the same time enhances his love for his wife. The physical relations they have make him appreciate her.

A wife, on the other hand, is reassured of her husband's love when they have physical relations. The act of sex relaxes her and lessens the stress in her life. Sex causes her to feel like a woman in the truest sense of the word.

Reasons for Sexual Difficulties

There are dangers involved with the sex life of couples. The following areas need attention in order to have good sexual relations:

1. Fatigue and Time Pressure

Life can get hectic. We are busy people. Sometimes, there's no time left for each other. People's sex drive remains intense, and the lack of attention can cause friction in the marriage. We may need to stop and pay attention to each other for a while.

2. Fear of Pregnancy

When couples are having regular sexual activity, there is the real possibility of pregnancy. Fear of having an unwanted or untimely pregnancy can discourage contact. This brings pressure to the relationship. Communication is the answer. Share your feelings, and then decide what you will do.

3. Extreme Modesty

Depending on how you were brought up and what moral standards you were taught, there could be a problem. The intimacy of the relationship could be stifled. Remember that marriage makes us one. There is no shame. We are free to please each other.

4. Poor Communication

Talking about sex is not always easy. It can be hard to communicate what we want and don't want. We need to be patient and understanding with each other. We want to give pleasure, not cause pain. Good communication is essential for good sex.

5. Poor Hygiene Habits

Before satisfying your sexual drives, you must be clean. Take a shower, brush your teeth, and take the necessary measures to be attractive to your mate. This is simply being considerate. Rushing the experience may be a turn-off, especially to your spouse.

How to Improve Your Love Life

1. Men Respond to Visual Cues

Wives need to understand this fact and use it in their relationship. They should be conscious of their figure and take care to dress for love in the bedroom. What a wife chooses to wear to bed can be a turn-on or a turn-off to her husband.

2. Women Respond to Touch and Talk

Husbands should learn to use phrases like "I love you" and "You are beautiful." Wives respond to passionate kisses and embraces. Husbands often want to rush the proceedings. Slow down and enjoy the ride. Your wife's excitement will be enhanced.

3. Aim to Please Your Mate

Sex is meant to satisfy our needs and drives, but that's not all there is to it. Sex is a way to give mutual pleasure. It's a great way to get to know one another.

> Let the husband render unto the wife due benevolence: and likewise also the wife unto the husband. (1 Corinthians 7:3)

Conclusion

Marriage is a fragile thing. Lots of things can go wrong. A successful, happy marriage is a result of two mature people loving each other. But it is also a relationship where problems are solved. Problems often arise in the areas of communication and sex. Accept them, anticipate them, and deal with them. You can win.

Next, we go on to the area of money in marriage.

Chapter Eight
Marriage and Money

Introduction

Money management is the third danger zone in marriage. We've discussed the dangers of poor communication and the dangers of sex in marriage. Now, we'll cover the area of money in marriage.

The goal of marriage is intimacy. There is no greater means of accomplishing this goal than managing money. Money in marriage can become your greatest nightmare, or it can become your greatest success. Someone said, "Your money is your life." Sharing your money, then, is effectively sharing your life.

Managing money is not easy, but it's not impossible. We may have to make some changes in how we handle our money. We want to make sure those changes are made according to the principles presented in the Bible.

The Biblical Concept of Money

The Bible tells us that everything belongs to God. He created everything, so He is the owner of everything.

If I were hungry, I would not tell thee: for the world
is mine, and the fullness there of. (Psalm 50:12)

We then are the stewards of God over the things He gives us,
including our money. We as stewards are accountable to Him.

Moreover it is required in stewards, that a man
be found faithful. (1 Corinthians 4:2)

In the Bible, God promises to meet our needs. He does not promise
to supply our "greeds." We have no reason to worry about money
or the lack of it.

But my God shall supply all you need according to his
riches in glory by Christ Jesus. (Philippians 4:19)

Money represents many dangers. We must be careful that money
does not become our master and we its servants.

But they that will be rich fall into temptation and a snare,
and into many foolish and hurtful lusts, which drown
men in destruction and perdition. (1 Timothy 6:9–10)

Contentment is the goal where money is concerned. Contentment
is being satisfied with what we have right now. When my wife and
I got our first apartment, all we had was a bed given to us by her
grandmother. We met in the middle of that bed every night because
it sagged so. We were just as happy then as we are now in our three-
bedroom house.

But godliness with contentment is great gain. For we
brought nothing in to this world, and it is certain we
can carry nothing out. And having food and raiment
let us be therewith content. (1 Timothy 6:6–8)

Proper money management is the basis of spiritual growth. In other words, the way we handle money is a reflection of our spiritual life. God will commit to our trust "true riches," but only if we handle our money properly. Our money is His money. We must be good managers of His money if we want His blessings.

He that is faithful in that which is least is faithful also in much; and he that is unjust in the least is unjust also in much. If therefore, ye have not been faithful in the unrighteous mammon, who will commit to your trust the true riches? (Luke 16:10–11)

The Biblical Nature of Money

The Bible presents a different perspective than the world on the value and proper use of money. We want to share several perspectives from the Bible about money.

First, Money Is Not Evil by Itself

Money is neutral. How we use it makes the difference. It is the love of money that's the problem. The love of money can lead us to difficulty. Money can be used to bring joy and happiness. It just depends on how we use it.

For the love of money is the root of all evil: which while some coveted after, they have erred from the faith and pierced themselves through with many sorrows. (1 Timothy 6:10)

Second, Money Does Not Last Long

Money tends to come and go; as fast as we make it, we spend it. When we were younger, my wife and I realized that whenever we got a little extra money, some unexpected expense would take it away. We always became a little uneasy when we had extra cash.

> Labour not to be rich: cease from thine own wisdom.
> Wilt thou set thine eyes upon that which is not? for
> riches certainly make themselves wings; they fly away
> as an eagle toward heaven. (Proverbs 23:4–5)

Thirdly, There Is Never Enough Money

No matter how much money you have, there are expenses that will eat it up. We also by nature want more and more. This depletes what we have. Contentment, therefore, is even more important in our financial dealings.

> He that loveth silver shall not be satisfied with silver; nor
> he that loveth abundance with increase: this is also vanity.
> When goods increase, they are increased that eat them;
> and what good is there to the owners thereof, save in the
> beholding of them with their eyes. (Ecclesiastes 5:10–11)

Fourth, with Money, It's Easy Come, Easy Go

Money that comes to us without labor is considered easy money. Gifts of money on a birthday or an anniversary are easily spent. It takes real discipline to keep free money. We often hear of those winning the lottery soon going bankrupt because "Easy come, easy go."

> Wealth gotten by vanity shall be diminished: but he that
> gathereth by labour shall increase. (Proverbs 13:11)

Finally, Money Can Be Used to Invest in Eternity

Money can be a powerful force for good. It can be made to last forever. If we use it to invest in that which is eternal, it can meet us on the other side. There are only two things that are eternal in this world: the Word of God and the souls of men. If we invest in getting the Word of God out to the world and in the salvation of souls, we're investing in eternity. As we think of the value and use of our money, we would do well to consider just what we do with it. We can use it for temporal needs or invest it in eternity.

> But lay up for yourselves treasures in heaven, where neither moth nor rust doth corrupt, and where thieves do not break through nor steal. (Matthew 6:20)

> Not that I desire a gift; but I desire fruit that may abound to your account. (Philippians 4:17)

Biblical Purposes of Money

God has given us four legitimate purposes for our money. We will share those purposes here.

1. Money Can Be Used to Provide for Our Needs

God has promised to meet all our needs as we continually serve Him. We must make sure we do not misspend God's provision on things we want but don't need.

> And having food and raiment let us be therewith content. (1 Timothy 6:8)

2. Money Can Be Used to Confirm God's Direction

God will direct our lives, if we allow Him to do so. One of the many ways God shows us His will is by providing the proper funds or withholding the money needed to do this or that. If a couple wants to buy a house, but they don't have the money for a down payment, the Lord may be saying, "No, not now." If you borrow the money and go ahead, you won't know this was the Lord's will. God could certainly provide the money if it's His will.

Rest in the LORD, and wait patiently for him: fret not thyself because of him who prospeth in his way, because of the man who bringeth wicked devices to pass. (Psalm 37:7)

3. Money Can Be Used to Meet the Needs of Others

God provides our needs. When He blesses us beyond our needs, we are to take the opportunity to help others that who are in need.

Let him that stole steal no more; but rather let him labour, working with his hands the thing which is good, that he may have to give to him that needeth. (Ephesians 4:28)

4. Money Can Be Used to Illustrate God's Power

God uses money to demonstrate His power. The world values money. For that reason, God often uses money to show the world what he can do. He may do a financial miracle on your behalf just to be a testimony to others around you. God provided my wife and me ten thousand dollars so we could work with military families in just this way. A church in Chicago sold their building for a hundred thousand dollars and divided the money among ten missionaries. God's power was demonstrated for all to see.

Bring ye all the tithes unto the storehouse, that there may
be meat in mine house, and prove me now here with, saith
the LORD of hosts, if I will not open you the windows
of heaven, and pour you out a blessing, that there shall
not be room enough to receive it. (Malachi 3:10)

We have been considering some general principles about money as
they are found in the Bible. Now we want to consider six principles
that have to do with married couples and their money.

Money Principles in Marriage

1. Hold All Assets in Common

Marriage intimacy calls for our money and bills to be held in
common. Don't have separate bank accounts, checking accounts,
or savings accounts. Don't have separate possessions. Houses, cars,
and other possessions are now ours, not his and hers.

Therefore shall a man leave his father and mother, and shall cleave
unto his wife; and they shall become one flesh. (Genesis 2:24)

2. Set Financial Goals Together

Married couples must learn to function as one unit. They should
decide together what to buy. They should decide together how much
to save and what to save for.

3. Serve God, Not Money

Money tends to control our lives. It can take the place of God in
our lives. We can look to money for our security. God is to be our
security. We want God to be in our marriage and in our finances.

No man can serve two masters; for either he will hate the one, and love the other; or else he will hold to the one, and despise the other. Ye cannot serve God and mammon. (Matthew 6:24)

4. Learn to Make Do

Most married couples start out with very little. Their parents may help them furnish an apartment with old furniture. Understand that your are not going to have, immediately, everything it took your parents years to accumulate. Be careful not go into debt. Debt is a financial trap.

5. Live Independent of In-Laws

Moms and dads usually want to help. If they want to help financially, let them help, but don't become dependent on them. The Bible says to leave and to cleave. We are to leave our parents and cleave to our mates, not our in-laws.

6. Make Financial Decisions Together

Before marriage, we make decisions about money on our own. When married, money becomes ours. Decisions on how we spend it are ours. A husband will do well to listen to his wife's counsel on money matters. God has given women a sense of intuition that men don't have. I once bought a used car after a test drive at night (the owner drove the car). I liked the design of the car. My wife, who knows nothing about cars, said no, and she was right. It was the biggest lemon we ever owned. Husbands are responsible for making final decisions, but they must realize the responsibility for those decisions are also theirs.

Finally, we want to list some money problem areas within marriage. Remember that money is one of the danger zones of marriage. These are the specific areas where trouble may originate.

Money Problem Areas

1. Communication

Couples must agree on their financial goals. When we were first married, my wife and I had no money problems. Of course, we had no money, but we had no problems. After we began to accumulate a little money, we had to decide what to do with it.

Financial goals can be divided into three areas: first, immediate goals, like food, clothing, and housing. Second, short-range goals, like things we desire down the road, things we'd like to have in the future, like a home of our own. The third area is long-range goals. We need to plan for retirement and leaving an inheritance to our children.

These goals should be planned together. Each one of these areas must be discussed and decided upon as you plan your future together. You need to come to a consensus as you decide what to do with every dollar. Three categories come to mind: spending, giving, and saving.

Spending

We must decide how much to spend. When my wife and I were first married, we had no TV. We saved a couple of hundred dollars and went to Sears. We found a TV we liked, but with taxes, it cost more than we had to spend. We tried to open a Sears charge account but had to wait a week to purchase anything with it. My wife said we should wait. I decided to buy the TV right then. We ate beans for a week but watched TV as we ate them.

Giving

We have to decide what we will give. The Bible requires a tithe. A tithe is 10 percent of our income. A tithe represents the whole. When a woman has a baby, she counts the fingers and toes. If there are ten of each, the baby is whole. Giving a tithe represents our belief that all we have belongs to God. This is a big decision, especially if your income is not large.

Saving

Saving requires financial discipline. Emergencies must be prepared for by saving a little each month. A couple should decide what percentage of their income they want to put aside each month. You can save for larger purchases, a car, or a house payment.

By the way, there are only three things you can do with your money: You can spend it, you can give it, or you can save it. Couples should do each one of these together.

2. Debt

A debt is something you owe. We can owe someone a favor. We can owe someone an apology. We can owe someone some money. Financially, debt can put great pressure on a marriage, especially if you can't pay what you owe.

> Owe no man any thing, but to love one another, for he that
> loveth another hath fulfilled the law. (Romans 13:8)

It is important for Christians in particular to pay the debts they owe. It's never right not to pay what we owe.

> The wicked borroweth, and payeth not again; but the
> righteous sheweth mercy and giveth. (Psalm 37:21)

The Problem with Debt

The Bible does not say debt is a sin, but it is dangerous. Debt puts you under the control of the lender.

> The rich rule over the poor, and the borrower is
> the servant to the lender. (Proverbs 22:7)

The Reason for Debt

We must be careful and watch out for get-rich-quick schemes. Remember that if something seems too good to be true, it usually is. Be careful of wanting something for nothing. Gambling is addictive. Don't let yourself get involved. Beware of playing the lottery. Don't be afraid of working for what you get.

> Wealth gotten by vanity shall be diminished: but he that
> gathereth by labour shall increase. (Proverbs 13:11)

Another reason people find themselves in debt is that they ignore their mate's financial input. Most couples pick an opposite for a mate: One is a spender, and the other is a saver. This is a counterbalance, not to be ignored.

The Way Out of Debt

Credit cards are usually the culprits when it comes to debt for young couples. It is tempting to get what we want without having to pay cash for it. Credit cards come with interest. The banks make money, unless you pay in full every month. Paying the minimum is designed to keep people in debt to the bank. Cut your credit cards.
If you have multiple cards, or other debts, pay the smallest debt first, and then add that to the next largest bill until all the debt is paid off. This is the snowball approach to getting out of debt.

If your debt is really large, you may be wise to sell what you don't need or can't afford. Selling an automobile with debt and purchasing one for cash may be prudent.

Money Management

Establish Roles

Remember your roles in marriage and practice them. The husband is the provider. He is responsible for supporting the family.

> But if any provide not for his own, and specially for
> those of his own house, he hath denied the faith,
> and is worse than an infidel. (1 Timothy 5:8)

A wife is not the breadwinner, but she can supplement the family income like the virtuous woman of Proverbs 31. Some wives who stay home with their children can work online and still care for the kids.

> She maketh fine linen, and selleth it, and deliverth
> girdles unto the merchant. (Proverbs 31:24)

The husband is responsible not only to make money but also to manage the money. Bills must be paid. This task can be delegated to the wife, but the responsibility is not hers.

Reasons Why Husbands Don't Manage the Money.

There are two basic reasons husbands resist managing their family's finances. First, the wife may have some insecurity when it comes to money. She may worry the bills won't get paid. Early in our marriage, my wife was allowed to take over the finances. She would pay all the bills immediately, even if we had no money left for food.

Second, a new husband may never have had to manage money before. His inexperience will make him resistant. After I bounced a few checks and missed paying some bills, I was ready to give it up. We have to learn the responsibilities we have.

Establish a Budget

To manage money in marriage, you need a budget. A budget is a spending plan. We must tell our money where to go, each month. If we don't tell it where to go, it will fly away. Most folks don't use a budget; you may have to find some help at your local bookstore or online to help you set up a budget.

We will suggest a simple budget here. You start with your gross income. After taxes and tithe, your remaining income is spendable income. Spendable income is divided three ways:

- 10 percent for savings
- 70 percent for expenses
- 20 percent for debt reduction and emergencies

> Then he said unto them, Render therefore unto Caesar the things which are Caesar's; and unto God the things that are God's. (Matthew 22:21)

And all the tithe of the land, whether of the seed or the land, or the fruit of the tree, is the LORD'S; it is holy unto the LORD. (Leviticus 27:19)

Conclusion

Money can make or break a marriage. Intimacy involves our finances. Sharing our income mutually makes us one in marriage. Handle your money correctly, and the chances for a successful marriage will increase.

CHAPTER NINE

The Components of a Christian Marriage

Introduction

A Christian marriage is characterized by Christian principles. We want to present those principles in this chapter. We will begin with a section defining a Christian marriage. After that, we will list the components that make a marriage a Christian marriage.

The Definition of a Christian Marriage

A Marriage of Believers

A Christian marriage is a marriage where both the husband and the wife are Christians. The Bible tells us that an "unequal yoke" is unacceptable in marriage. Christians should not marry unbelievers.

Be not unequally yoked together with unbelievers: for what
fellowship hath righteousness with unrighteousness and what
communion hath light with darkness. (2 Corinthians 6:14)

If two unbelievers are married and one becomes a believer, the
believer is to stay with the unbeliever. This is in the hope that the
influence of the believing mate may cause the unbeliever to come
to believe in Christ.

And the woman, which hath an husband that believeth not,
and if he be pleased to dwell with her, let her not leave him.
For the unbelieving husband is sanctified by the wife, and the
unbelieving wife is sanctified by the husband; else were your
children unclean; but now are they holy. (1 Corinthians 7:13–14)

A Marriage Committed to Christ

To be a Christian marriage, both husband and wife must be
committed to the Lordship of Christ. Each one must be in submission
to the Lord's will and responsive to His direction.

And why call ye me, Lord, Lord, and do
not what I say? (Luke 6:46)

A Marriage Based on Biblical Principles

A Christian marriage is a marriage ordered by the Word of God.
The most obvious principle is, first, the husband must love his wife.

Husbands love your wives, even as Christ also loved the
church: and gave himself for it. (Ephesians 5:25)

Second, the wife must be in submission to her husband. She must
yield to his loving leadership.

Wives submit yourselves unto your own husbands,
as unto the Lord. (Ephesians 5:22)

A Marriage Where Biblical Roles Are Played

The Fourfold Role of the Husband

1. He Is to Be the Provider

> But if any provide not for his own, and especially
> those of his own house, he hath denied the faith,
> and is worse than an infidel. (1 Timothy 5:8)

2. He Is to Be the Protector

> For the husband is the head of the wife, even as Christ
> is the saviour of the body. (Ephesians 5:22)

3. He Is to Be the Lover

> Husbands, love your wives, even as Christ also loved the
> church, and gave himself for it. (Ephesians 5:23)

4. He Is to Be the Leader

> For the husband is the head of the wife, even as Christ
> is the head of the church. (Ephesians 5:23)

The Fourfold Role of the Wife

1. She Is to Be a Helper

And the LORD God said, It is not good that the man should
be alone: I will make him an help meet for him. (Genesis 2:18)

1. She Is to Be a Keeper (at Home)

To be discreet, chaste, keepers at home, good,
obedient to their own husbands, that the word
of God be not blasphemed. (Titus 5:22)

3. She Is to Be a Follower

Wives, submit yourselves unto your own husbands,
as unto the Lord. (Ephesians 5:22)

4. She Is to Be a Counselor (Advisor)

Two are better than one: because they have a good
reward for their labour. (Ecclesiastes 4:9)

The Components of a Christian Marriage

Salvation

A Christian marriage is composed of a husband and a wife who are
both saved by grace through faith in the Lord Jesus.

Sirs, what must I do to be saved? And they said,
Believe on the Lord Jesus Christ, and thou shalt
be saved, and thy house. (Acts 16:30–31)

Priesthood of the Husband

In the family, the spiritual leader is to be the husband. He serves as
a priest in the family. The ministry of the priest is to present God to
the people and the people to God. The husband presents the family
to God and God to the family.

But ye are a chosen generation, a royal priesthood,
a holy nation, a peculiar people. (1 Peter 2:9)

Church Attendance

The church is the body of Christ. The church meets for worship, fellowship, and instruction in the Word of God. Attending church is a component of a Christian marriage. That church must teach the doctrines of the Bible and reinforce the standards of biblical separation.

Not forsaking the assembling of ourselves together, as the manner of some is; but exhorting one another; and so much the more, as ye see the day approaching. (Hebrews 10:25)

Spiritual Discipline

Spiritual disciplines are the practices that cause us to grow in Christ. They include prayer, Bible study, and fellowship with other Christians. The husband and wife should practice these disciplines personally and together.

But grow in grace, and in the knowledge of our
Lord and Saviour Jesus Christ. (2 Peter 3:18)

Christian Environment

A Christian marriage must involve a wholesome home environment that includes wholesome music and wholesome language. It must be free of unwholesome books and magazines.

A Christian home is one where the television and the computer and the cell phones are controlled and censored. The Christian home should be a little bit of heaven on earth.

CHAPTER TEN
Romance in Marriage

Introduction

Someone once said, "Love is a many-splendored thing." Love is expressed in many ways. Love, then, has many expressions. Here are five ways we may experience love.

1. Puppy Love

The earliest expression of love takes place in our youth. Puppy love is often filled with infatuation. We have fond memories about those who caught our attention as we were just starting out.

2. Married Love

Married love involves someone we want to spend the rest our lives with. This love is exclusive. It centers on one person. It is a sacrificial love.

3. Maternal Love

This is the love we have for our children. A mother's love is amazing. It brings a bond that lasts a lifetime. Fathers experience paternal love for their children, as well.

4. Christian Love

Love was expressed by God when He sent His Son into the world to become a sacrifice for our sins. God's love is shared when we accept Christ as our Savior from sin. His love is placed in our hearts by the Holy Spirit.

5. Romantic Love

Romance involves the expression of love for a mate. Solomon wrote of this kind of love in his Old Testament book, the Song of Solomon.

Romantic Love Defined

Romantic love is the expression of true love. It involves the tender feeling a man and a woman have for each other. Those emotions cause us to care for one another and want to be with one another for a lifetime. Both men and women are subject to these feelings, but women are usually more sensitive to romance than men. Ladies will watch the Hallmark Channel and the Lifetime Channel on television. When they are not watching TV, they are reading romance novels. Men are not so enthusiastic about romance, especially after they are married. Their interest is in their work and perhaps sports. Men have to work at cultivating romantic love.

The Importance of Romantic Love

Romantic Love and the Wife

Romantic love to a wife is like water to a plant. With it, she flourishes; without it, she wilts. Romance after marriage assures a wife of her husband's love. It constitutes a need in her life. Denying her romantic love is cruel.

Romantic Love and the Husband

The one responsible for the expression of romantic love in marriage is the husband. The scripture commands husbands to love their wives.

> Husbands, love your wives, even as Christ also loved the
> church, and gave himself for it. (Ephesians 5:25)

Romantic love is an emotion, a feeling. You don't want to lose that loving feeling. It must be cultivated in the wife. Flowers and candy are often useful in cultivating this kind of love. These gifts tell your wife you still love her.

Romantic love is inspired by the wife. As a husband contemplates the features that originally captured his attention, his expression of love becomes easier. Contemplating the charm of her personality, her femininity, and other qualities leads to expressions of romantic love. These expressions can be as simple as a word or a touch. They may result in acts of sacrifice or sensitivity to her needs. Romance is a biblical concept.

Romance Expressed through Romantic Environments

1. Fragrances

> 2. Because of the savour of thy good ointments
> thy name is as ointment poured forth, therefore do
> the virgins love thee. (Song of Solomon 1:3)

2. Flowers

> My beloved is gone down into his garden, to the beds
> of spices, to feed in the gardens and to gather lilies. I

am my beloved's, and my beloved is mine: he feedeth
among the lilies. (Song of Solomon 6:2–3)

3. Foods

He brought me to the banqueting house, and his
banner over me is love. (Song of Solomon 2:3)

4. Jewelry

Thy cheeks are comely with rows of jewels, thy neck
with chains of gold. (Song of Solomon 1:10)

5. Beautiful Scenery

Come, my beloved, let us go forth into the field; let
us lodge in the villages. Let us get up early to the vine
yards; let us see if the vine flourish, whether the tender
grape appear, and the pomegranates bud forth: there will
I give thee my loves. (Song of Solomon 7:11–12)

Romance Expressed through Romantic Actions

1. Kisses

Let him kiss me with kisses of his mouth, for thy
love is better than wine. (Song of Solomon 1:2)

2. Embraces

His left hand is under my head, and his right hand
doeth embrace me. (Song of Solomon 2:63)

3. Displays of Manliness

Who is this that cometh out of the wilderness like pillars
of smoke perfumed with myrrh and frankincense, with
all powers of the merchant? (Song of Solomon 3:6)

King Solomon made himself a chariot of the
wood of Lebanon. (Song of Solomon 3:9)

Romance Is Expressed through Romantic Language

1. His Description of Her

Behold, thou art fair, my love; behold, thou art fair; thou hast
doves' eyes with in thy locks; thy hair is as a flock of goats,
that appear from Mount Gilead. (Song of Solomon 4:1–7)

2. Her Description of Him

My beloved is white and ruddy. The chiefest among ten
thousand. His head is as the most fine gold; his locks are
bushy, and black as a raven. (Song of Solomon 5:10–16)

3. The Language of Love

Thou hast ravished my heart, my sister, my spouse; thou hast
ravished my heart with one of thine eyes, with one chain of
thy neck. How fair is thy love, my sister, my spouse! How
much better is thy love than wine! and the smell of thine
ointments than all spices. (Song of Solomon 4:8–15)

Conclusion

Romantic love is the fire that keeps marriage exciting. In our busy age, we often neglect the effort it takes to be romantic. Romantic love is a necessity for a wife. Husbands need to be reminded of this essential need.

CHAPTER ELEVEN
Divorce and Remarriage

Introduction

With some trepidation, we come to the subject of divorce and remarriage. We want to address this subject from a biblical perspective. The Bible recognizes divorce. Jesus said it was allowed because of the "hardness of their hearts." Divorce was not (and is still not) in God's plan for marriage. Remarriage is also forbidden by scripture. Divorce should be avoided, especially by the believer. But statistics show that the divorce rate among Christians is just about equal to the overall divorce rate in America.

We want to share the truth of the scripture about divorce and remarriage, trusting that the truth will set us free. Our hope is that your marriage will last a lifetime, guided by the principles of God's Word.

The Prevalence of Divorce

Today, 40 to 50 percent of those who walk down the aisle wind up in court to get a divorce. Nearly half of all those who marry will divorce. Those are not good percentages. Second marriages have a 70 percent chance of failure, and third marriages have even a higher rate of failure. Why is this true? The biggest reason for divorce is not adultery, cruelty, desertion, or neglect. It is the claim of incompatibility. Folks just decide that they can't get along with one another. Past generations were required to remain married and work out their differences. Now the courts are not so strict and will allow divorce for almost any reason.

The Definition of Divorce

Webster's defines divorce as "the legal and formal dissolution of a marriage." Divorce, biblically, is the human division of what God has joined together.

> Wherefore they are no more twain but one flesh.
> What therefore God hath joined together, let
> not man put asunder. (Matthew 19:6)

The Problem with Divorce

Divorce is wrong for seven biblical reasons.

1. God Hates Divorce

> For the LORD, the God of Israel, saith that he
> hateth putting away. (Malachi 2:16)

God invented marriage. He meant it to be a lifelong relationship. Divorce is our attempt at ending a marriage prematurely.

2. Divorce Strikes at the Foundation of Society

> If the foundation be destroyed, what can
> the righteous do? (Psalm 11:3)

The family is the foundation of society. Divorce destroys the foundation. Families are broken, and children are left to handle the circumstances of parents living separately, destroying their security.

3. Divorce Is the Result of the Hardness of Man's Heart

> He saith unto them, Moses because of the hardness of
> your hearts suffered you to put away your wives; but
> from the beginning it was not so. (Matthew 19:8)

Hardness of the heart smacks of rebellion. It means an unwillingness to do marriage God's way. It is a refusal to accept God's teaching and standards for marriage.

4. Divorce Causes Children to Choose Sides

> No man can serve two masters; for either he will hate the one,
> and love the other; or else he will hold to the one, and despise
> the other. Ye can not serve God and mammon. (Matthew 6:24)

This verse is a direct teaching about the mastery of money, but the principle of dual authority is also applicable here. Divorce sets up a dual authority between mother and father. Children are forced to choose who they will obey. This affects their security and can lead to bitterness.

5. Divorce Requires Christians to Go to Court

> Dare any of you, having a matter against another, go to law
> before the unjust, and not before the saints? (1 Corinthians 6:1)

Christians should not take other Christians to court. It is a bad testimony before the world to drag our disagreements and offences before an unsaved judge. Divorce requires legal action. God's children should not be involved in the justice system of the world.

6. Divorce Does Not End Marriage

> For the woman which hath an husband is bound by the law to her husband so long as he liveth: but if her husband be dead, she is loosed from the law of her husband. (Romans 7:2)

This is the reason we take vows in marriage that say "til death do us part." Marriage is not for eternity, but for life. Divorce will end a marriage legally, but only death can end a marriage biblically.

7. Divorce Mars the Image of Christ and the Church

> For we are members of his body, of his flesh, and of his bones. For this cause shall a man leave his father and mother, and shall be joined unto his wife, and they two shall be one flesh. This is a great mystery: but I speak concerning Christ and the church. (Ephesians 5:30–32)

God has chosen to use marriage as the image of Christ and His church. Divorce, especially by Christians, stains that image. Marriage and the relationship of Christ and the church are to mirror permanence.

The Grounds for Divorce

Divorce may be granted in the United States on different grounds, depending on the state. There are two forms of divorce: fault divorce and no-fault divorce. The first type of divorce covers issues like adultery and abuse. No-fault divorce is for reasons like incompatibility. The Bible offers no grounds for divorce.

And he answered and said unto them, Have ye not read
that he which made them at the beginning made them
male and female, and said, For this cause shall a man
leave father and mother, and shall cleave to his wife: and
they twain shall be one flesh? Wherefore they are no more
twain, but one flesh. What therefore God hath joined
together, let no man put asunder. (Matthew 19:4–6)

God intended marriage to be a lifelong relationship. The marriage
vows say as much: "for richer, for poorer, in sickness and in health,
until death do us part." Marriage can be broken only by death.

For the woman which hath an husband is bound by the law to
her husband so long as he liveth; but if the husband be dead,
she is loosed from the law of her husband. (Romans 7:2)

Now we want to address the issue of what has become known as the
exception clause as stated by the Lord Jesus.

And I say unto you, whosoever shall put away his wife,
except it be for fornication, and shall marry another,
committeth adultery: and whoso marrieth her which is
put away doth commit adultery. (Matthew 19:9)

Two words here are important to understand. Adultery is committed
by married people who have sexual relations with someone other
than their mate. Fornication includes adultery but is a general term
for all deviant sexual activity. This includes homosexuality and
same-sex marriages. We believe that Jesus was referring to same-sex
marriage, which is condemned in the scripture.

Thou shalt not lie with mankind, as with woman
kind, it is abomination. (Leviticus 18:22)

Regulations of Divorce

Although the Bible does not condone divorce or remarriage for any reason, we are given some regulations in 1 Corinthians 7.

First, Christians are not to initiate divorce. Nonbelievers may sue for divorce, and no resistance in that case is recommended.

> And to the married I command, yet not I, but the Lord, Let
> not the wife depart from her husband. (1 Corinthians 7:10)

Second, Christians need not resist being divorced by nonbelievers. If the nonbeliever chooses to stay with the believer, the marriage should be preserved.

> But if the unbelieving depart, let him depart. A brother
> or a sister is not under bondage in such cases, but
> God hath called us to peace. (1 Corinthians 7:1)

Third, Christians who divorce have two options. They must remain unmarried or be reconciled to their mates.

> But and if she depart, let her remain unmarried,
> or be reconciled to her husband: and let not the
> husband put away his wife. (1 Corinthians 7:1)

The reason the divorced person is to remain unmarried is that Jesus said remarriage would constitute adultery.

> And I say unto you, whoso ever shall put away his
> wife, except for fornication, and shall marry another,
> committeth adultery; and who so marrieth her which is
> put away doth commit adultery. (Matthew 19:19)

Fourth, Christians are to remain in a marriage with an unbeliever if the unbeliever wants to remain in the relationship. The reason the believer should stay in the marriage is for the possible salvation of the unsaved mate and for the salvation of the children.

> And the woman which hath an husband that believeth not, and if he be pleased to dwell with her let her not leave him. For the unbelieving husband is sanctified by the wife, and unbelieving wife is sanctified by the husband; either were your children unclean, but now they are holy. (1 Corinthians 7:13–14)

Fifth, Christians can remarry upon the death of their spouse but only to another Christian and, of course, only to someone who has not been divorced.

> The wife is bound by the law as long as her husband liveth; but if her husband be dead, she is at liberty to be married to whom she will; but only in the Lord. (1 Corinthians 7:39)

Finally, the Christian who has divorced and remarried should stay in that marriage. Adultery is a forgivable sin. It would make no sense to end the marriage. The verse I will use to confirm this truth may not specifically mention marriage, but I believe the principle covers marriage.

> Let every man abide in the same calling where in he was called. (1 Corinthians 7:20)

Avoidance of Divorce

I want to make some suggestions as to how to avoid divorce and maintain a successful marriage. Here are five things we can do to preserve our marriages:

1. Remember Your Vows

Today, the old-fashioned marriage vows are not as universal as they once were. The vows that include the words "for better, for worse, in sickness and health, until death do us part" are Bible-based vows fitting for a Christian marriage. Vows form a lifelong covenant. We need to do all we can to keep those vows.

2. Rebuild Your Relationship with the Lord

Trouble in marriage often comes from a backslidden relation with the Lord. That relationship needs to be restored. This can be done by confessing our sin and recommitting to the basics of Christian life: Bible study, prayer, and church attendance. Renew your love for one another. You may need to put a little romance back into your marriage. Take more time for one another. Express you love, and it will return to you.

3. Realize the Need for Counsel

Not all advice is good advice. But the Bible says, "There is safety in a multitude of counselors." Take counsel from a godly person with a good marriage. Most pastors are able to give marital counsel.

4. Review Your Understanding of a Biblical Marriage

This is the purpose of writing this book. I wanted to help couples having difficulty by writing a book explaining what the Bible says about marriage. By reading this book, you will see what a biblical marriage looks like.

5. Regard the Lord as Capable of Saving Your Marriage

God is not finished with us yet. He can do the impossible. He can change our hearts. We must trust the Lord to be able to save us from a difficult situation.

Conclusion

We pray for all Christians who are contemplating divorce. I encourage you to follow the biblical pattern for marriage. Your happiness and the stability of your children depend on your faithfulness to God's Word.

Addendum

How to Find a Mate

Seven Deal Breakers and Seven Game Changers

Dedication

I would like to dedicate this addendum to my five grandchildren.

At this time, these young people are finishing high school and entering college. They will need God's guidance in finding mates. My hope is that they will understand and follow these principles of marriage.

My prayer is that God will give each one of them Christian mates, as he did for me, and as he did for their parents.

My further hope is that the counsel I give to my grandchildren will also be received by other Christians as they search for their mates.

Introduction

Before I leave the subject of marriage, I want to give some attention to how to find a mate.

> Whoso findeth a wife findeth a good thing and
> obtaineth favour of the Lord. (Proverbs 18:22)

This verse indicates that "mates" are to be found. This search will involve the use of biblical principles. I am using the terms "Deal

Breakers" (negative principles) and "Game Changers" (positive principles) to address this search for a mate. I have listed seven Deal Breakers and seven Game Changers.

My purpose is to help people find the mate God has for them.

Seven Deal Breakers

1. Your Mate Must Be a Believer

> The scripture is very clear on this issue: Christians must marry another Christian. It's not enough to be moral or religious. Jesus said, "Ye must be born again." We must accept Christ as our Savior from sin, trusting his work on the cross to be the only way to heaven.

> Jesus saith unto him, I am the way, the truth, and the life, no man cometh unto the Father, but by me. (John 14:6)

The scripture warns of an "unequal yoke." Two oxen were yoked together to plow a field. An unequal yoke would be an oxen and a horse tied together to pull the plow. In marriage, a saved person and an unsaved person would be an unequal yoke.

> Be ye not unequally yoked together with unbelievers; for what fellowship hath righteousness with unrighteousness? and what communion hath light with darkness? (2 Corinthians 6:14)

2. Your Mate Must Be in God's Will

God's will is paramount for the Christian. Even Jesus said, when speaking to His Father, "Not my will, but thine be done." If your choice of a mate is not God's will, then that's a Deal Breaker. How do you know if someone is in His will? The greatest guide to God's will is His peace.

> Let the peace of God rule in your hearts, to the which also ye are called in one body, and be ye thankful. (Colossians 3:15)

Peace must "rule" in your heart as an indicator of God's will. The word *rule* means to officiate, to referee. Peace is the quiet confidence that this is the right decision. Peace must rule in your quest for a mate.

As I was considering if it was God's will for me to ask my wife to marry me, I experienced God's perfect peace. I was on the fantail (back end of the ship) of the USS *Forrestal*. It was late at night, the stars were shining, and I was praying. God's peace settled over my heart, and I knew without a doubt that this was God's will.

3. Your Mate Must Be Approved by Your Parents

God works through a chain of command. God uses this method to communicate His will in every area of life. There is a chain of command in the family. It begins with God, then Christ, the husband, the wife, and then the children.

> But I would have you to know, that the head of every man is Christ, and the head of the woman is the man; and the head of Christ is God. (1 Corinthians 11:3)

In the family, God works through the parents to the children. The order continues to work regardless of age. Parental approval of our choice of a mate is conformation of God's will. If parents on either side are disapproving, you should wait and reconsider your choice or its timing. If they approve, you have God's confirmation of your choice.

4. Your Mate Must Be Going Your Way

Can two walk together, except they be agreed? (Amos 3:3)

The Old Testament prophet, Amos, asks a telling question, one that should be asked of every person wanting to get married. The question is, "Do you and your intended mate have the same goals? Are you going in the same direction, at the same time?"

He keepeth the paths of judgment, and preserveth
the way of his saints. (Proverbs 2:8)

For the ways of man are before the eyes of the LORD,
and he pondereth all his goings. (Proverbs 5:21)

All of us have a certain path that God has ordained for us. It might be a certain career path or even the ministry. Whatever it may be, our mate should be headed in the same direction.

When I met my wife, she was headed to Columbia Bible College. I was in the Navy, but I was getting a cut in my enlistment time in order to go to Moody Bible Institute. We did not know just where we would end up, but we were headed in the same direction.

5. Your Mate Must Hold the Same Standards

Wherefore come out from among them, and be ye
separate. saith the Lord, and touch not the unclean
thing: and I will receive you. (2 Corinthians 6:17)

This verse indicates that you should have standards of practice in your Christian life. This has to do with doctrines and actions that are acceptable, according to your faith. While your beliefs and practices don't have to match perfectly, the closer they are, the less friction there will be.

The fundamentals of Christian doctrine held by each person should be the same. Doctrines like the deity of Christ and salvation by faith should be held by both candidates for marriage.
If you don't agree on the "deadly Ds" (drinking, drugs, and dancing), you may not want to get married. There are many other issues that may be Deal Breakers in this area.

You may think these issues unimportant, but over the long haul of marriage, they can be a wedge that makes staying together difficult.

6. Your Mate Must Be Free to Marry

What would disqualify someone from being a choice for marriage? The Bible, God's Word, is clear as to who is free to marry and who is not.

> And I say unto you, whosoever shall put away his wife, except it be for fornication, and shall marry another, committeth adultery: and whoso marrieth her which is put away doth commit adultery. (Matthew 19:9)

One who is divorced (put away) and remarries commits adultery. And likewise, whoever they marry commits adultery. If someone is divorced, they are given two choices.

> And unto the married I command yet not I, but the Lord, let not the wife depart from her husband; but if she depart let her remain unmarried, or be reconciled to her husband; and let not the husband put away his wife. (1 Corinthians 7:10–11)

The rule is, the divorced person is not a candidate for marriage. They are not free to marry someone else, unless their mate is deceased.

> The wife is bound by the law as long as her husband liveth, but if her husband be dead, she is at liberty to be married to whom she will; only in the Lord. (1 Corinthians 7:39)

7. Your Mate Must Be Willing to Marry

With divorce so prevalent in our society, many young people are opting to live together without getting married. Living together does not constitute a marriage. In fact, it is a matter of fornication. Fornication, of course, is a sin.

If your intended mate refuses to marry and be recognized by the state and God, you should not continue in the relationship. This should be a Deal Breaker.

Seven Game Changers

1. Ask the Lord to Lead You

> Prayer is paramount when looking for a mate. While prayer is not twisting God's arm, He does respond to prayer, if it's according to His will.

> Young lions do lack, and suffer hunger: but they that seek the LORD shall not want any good thing. (Psalm 34:10)

> Ask, and it shall be given you; seek, and ye shall find; knock, and it shall be opened unto you. (Matthew 7:7)

Prayer is a Game Changer. The scripture says, "Ye have not because ye ask not." If you want to find a mate, ask God.

2. Wait on the Lord

Wait on the LORD: be of good courage, and he shall strengthen thine heart; wait, I say, on the LORD. (Psalm 27:14)

Once you have prayed and made your request known to the Lord, you must be willing to wait on His timing.

The question is, what do we do while we wait? The answer is, you begin working, not to find the right one but to *be* the right one.

You should begin to work on several areas:

- physically: work on diet and exercise
- spiritually: read the Bible, attend Bible studies
- socially: attend church and build your social skills
- career: improve your knowledge and work skills

Finding a mate is sometimes a matter of stumbling over them in the pathway of duty.

3. Be Sure You Are in God's Will

The greatest place to be is right in the center of God's will for your life. Make sure you stay in God's will, if you want to find a mate. Stay diligent. Stay pure.

Decisions must be made according to God's Word and confirmed by God's peace. If you want to find God's will for your mate, you must stay in God's will for your life.

For ye have need of patience, that, after ye have done the will of God, ye might receive the promise. (Hebrews 10:36)

4. Decide Where You Are Going

If you don't know where you're going, you shouldn't ask someone to go with you.

Can two walk together, except they be agreed? (Amos 3:3)

Coming out of high school or college, you must decide what you want to do with the rest of your life. It may be a career path or some form of ministry. You should ask God and your parents for direction.

When you find the path for you, then and only then should you ask someone to go with you.

In all thy ways acknowledge him, and he shall direct thy paths. (Proverbs 3:6)

5. Look for Someone with a Servant's Heart

One of the greatest qualities of character anyone can have is a servant's heart. This is a quality possessed by the Lord Jesus, and one He recommended to His disciples.

For even the son of man came not to be ministered unto, but to minister, and to give his life a ransom for many. (Mark 10:45)

But he that is greatest among you shall be your servant. (Matthew 23:11)

This quality was found in Rebekah, who became the wife of Isaac. Abraham's servant, having been sent to find a wife for Isaac, asked the Lord to indicate who it was by an act of service. Rebekah not only gave him a drink of water but offered water to all his camels.

Learning to serve others is a mark of maturity. It serves married couples well because husbands and wives must put their spouse's needs ahead of their own.

6. Seek Someone of an Opposite Temperament

Online dating services match folks who are compatible. It's not wrong for a married couple to share the same interests, but the Bible indicates the necessity of being different. When God created Eve for Adam, he intended them to fulfill each other's needs. He didn't clone Eve, or it would have been Adam and Steve rather than Adam and Eve.

> And the LORD God said, it is not good for man to be alone: I will make a help meet for him. (Genesis 2:18)

Adam and Eve were to have opposite qualities that would meet their different needs. In marriage, these qualities become obvious: One is a spender, the other is a saver; one is outgoing, the other is a loner; one is a perfectionist, and the other is less rigid. These polar opposites tend to balance out one another. If they were both the same, one would not be needed.

7. List What You Want in a Mate

This may seem like an exercise in futility, but I have some scripture that may change your mind:

> Delight thyself also in the Lord; and he shall give thee the desires of thine heart. (Psalm 37:4)

Before I met my wife, I sat down and made a list of what I wanted in a spouse. I listed several things liked: I wanted a girl with a profession; she was a secretary. I wanted someone who dressed professionally; she wore suits and heels. I wanted someone serving the Lord; she worked with children at church and was a Christian camp counselor. I wanted someone who was attractive; she was an auburn-haired beauty.

God was true to His promise. I concentrated on serving Him, and He gave me the desire of my heart.

Conclusion

I believe God has a mate for everyone, with very few exceptions. In your search for a spouse, there are both Deal Breakers and Game Changers to be considered. If you order your search, avoiding the Deal Breakers and observing the Game Changers, I believe you'll have success. Success is finding a mate you can spend the rest of your life with, while raising a family to serve the Lord.

Printed in the United States
By Bookmasters